RETURN TO THE
LIGHT WITHIN

Return to The Light Within

How I Woke Up, Rediscovered Who I Am,
and Found Happiness

Return to The Light Within

How I Woke Up, Rediscovered Who I Am, and Found Happines

By Dmitria Burby

Published by Luminance Press

Lake Oswego, OR

www.dmitriaburby.com

1st Edition, September 2021

ISBN 978-1-7370486-0-2 (ebook)

ISBN 978-1-7370486-1-9

Cover design by: Anna Svistun

Interior design by: Hamza Azeem

Printed in the United States

Disclaimer

This book is a memoir. It reflects the author's present recollections of experiences over time. Some names and characteristics have been changed, some events have been compressed, and some dialogue has been recreated.

Dedication

This book is dedicated with love to my family:

My Husband, Jason, who shows infinite support for everything I do, no matter how crazy it may seem.

To my children, for inspiring me with your own light that you shine in the world each day.

To my parents and sisters, for helping shape my experiences so I could become who I am today.

To Aaron, for showing me the power and expansive love that can come from losing someone you love.

Acknowledgments

No one transforms, evolves, or grows on their own. Yes, each individual has to make the commitment and put in their own work, but each of us also have important teachers, helpers and guides along the way.

Thank you to my shamanic guides and teachers that have and continue to illuminate my path, hold me, and nourish me. While not named here, you know who you are. I truly believe you are divine gifts in my life.

Thank you to my husband, Jason, who encourages me when I question myself, pushes me when I am complacent, and continues to be my biggest cheerleading in my life. Thank you for being my partner in everything that we do and teaching me life's greatest lesson along the way, how to enjoy life.

To my children with their almost infinite patience, thank you. I know that there were many times when I would get lost in the depths of writing and you were always there to remind me of what is most important in life, which is true connection and relationships.

To my parents and sisters, you created my foundation in life. I am deeply grateful for all of our shared memories. I would never be here, in this place of wonder, without experiencing

y unique childhood. Mom and Dad, thank you for the
crifices you made to give me the opportunities I have had
my life. I see them and I appreciate them deeply. Sisters,
ank you for living life side by side and agreeing to navigate
is lifetime as blood.

ank you to all of my friends and acquaintances for having
e conversations that sparked wonder in me to dive even
eper into my own work and evolve.

ank you to my editorial team that supported me as I
rthed this book into the world. I am honored that Scott
d Bethany chose to support my idea and give part of
emselves to bring this work into the world. It is because of
eir dedication to the craft that this truly is a book.

Table of
Contents

Author's Note

Thank you. Those two words cannot possibly convey the gratitude that I have for you picking up and reading this book. I don't take it lightly that you are spending your precious time reading my journey. Please know that I have written these words with love and honesty infused in each of them. I worked to share experiences I have had to the best of my ability, even when it felt like something might be too much to share or that some parts might inspire skepticism.

I open myself up in the rawest and most vulnerable way I know how to show you the layers of me, what lies at my core. I do this so you can see into me, see what I am made of, and know what you are made of too. My greatest hope is that you are able to connect with some or all of my journey to help you in yours. Not to follow in my footsteps, but to find context and some footing in a land that can feel unknown and confusing at times. To illuminate the possibilities available for you to discover.

This book is what I would call divinely inspired. While I have had past musings about writing a book, if you would have asked me even just a few months ago if I was going to write a book, my answer would have been a resounding, "No!" But here we are, after weeks upon weeks of writing that just didn't want to stop until every part of me was poured out on paper. I am trusting that there must be a reason that Spirit wanted this story shared. I am trusting in that plan and following my path of true joy. I hope that you do too.

A brief note: Throughout this book I reference Divine, the Universe, Spirit, and I'm sure a few other names interchangeably. What I mean to reference is source energy, the thing that everything else was created from. Whatever your religious affiliation or spiritual beliefs, when I'm using these terms I'm referring to the highest source that you believe in. I believe that, no matter what name you use to reference that highest source, they are all ultimately pointing to the same thing. I personally struggle to name "it" and so tend to reference that original Divine Spirit with many names.

I want to thank you in advance for the grace you are giving me by following my story, as I sometimes struggle to translate the knowing and feeling inside of me into a logical flow of words. I hope that you enjoy reading about my journey as much as I have enjoyed experiencing and writing the transformation myself. I hope that it opens your eyes to something new, planting seeds of love, hope, and inspiration somewhere deep inside of you where you need and want it most. I also hope that you question some of it, so that you can explore new realms and dimensions of your own, so that you can ultimately find your own truth and knowing.

As you explore my journey from having it all: a successful career, loving husband, beautiful children, the house and cars, to the realization that I was disconnected and unhappy, and finally into a deeply spiritual journey of my awakening, you will hopefully find moments that resonate with you. You are sure to encounter other moments that feel a little "out there." Ground yourself in your own knowing and be open to the possibilities as I shed the masks that I held in place for so long, revealing what is accessible to all of us when we embark on this path inward. So much love and light to you on your sacred journey.

CHAPTER 1

The New Earth

Being someone who has never been able to keep a surprise secret, I'll just jump right to the pinnacle of this story. What I discovered is that I am a Divine Spirit.

(Bear with me as I explain how I got to this place. I know that, if you are anything like I was at the beginning of my journey, this is the point in the story where I would check out and move on to read literally anything else.)

I have thought of myself as *ancient* Divine Spirit, but when you exist in a place with no time or space, can you really describe yourself with adjectives related to time?

I have come to know that I am Divine Spirit (and so are you). That probably feels like a gigantic leap, moving from being lost and barely knowing who I was to making a bold statement like that. But that is what this journey is all about. The journey is about rediscovering who and what we are, rekindling the spark that is still alive inside of us, no matter how many layers of material life and matrix (societal) rules we have piled on top of it. What I discovered is that, no matter how lost we feel, that spark continues to exist, we just have to have the desire to find it again. And when we find it, we have to have the commitment to protect it and cultivate it.

I believe that we leave a wonderful place where time and space do not exist to come to Earth to have human experiences. We come here and create all that we create because it is the opposite of the existence that we normally relate to. Imagine a time-space continuum, a dimension where everything is perfect and harmonious. Imagine a place where the light is soft and infused into everything, like the first moments of the sunrise when the light gently bathes nature in soft pinkness. Imagine that there is only love here; it is the dimension, the realm of Spirits. The dimension of the god(s) and goddess(es). In this dimension of love, where everything is perfection, what could there possibly be a desire for? The only desire there could possibly be is a desire to expand, to grow, and to become more. To create more and more love. The best that I have been able to figure out is that we are pure Divine love and that love is created as our spirit expands and grows.

So in the midst of the mist of Divine perfection, there is a desire to grow and expand further out into the infinite universe, beyond where we have been before. To do this, our spirits make the choice to come to this Earth dimension. We are the brave that are willing to give up the comfort of what I'll call "home." We have come to experience the excitement, the highs and the lows of living in this place. We come here and live alongside wars, hate, murder, famine, and so many more of the atrocities that humanity creates. We come and are willing to experience the tragedies of our own humanity so that we can return to love with our hearts expanded. We return with the ability to feel and create more love than when we arrived.

You may ask if this is true for everybody. You may even have someone specific you are thinking of, that someone who you think could not possibly be following this path of expansion of only love. But I promise you, even though it might not make sense to you or I in the moment, they are here, doing the work too. They don't even need to know it and, honestly, they probably are not aware of the vast amount of love in the universe. They might even be one who is inflicting pain on others. They are still expanding the universal love.

I don't know all the details of how this works. I just know that it does. I know that, when we die and leave our human bodies, we encounter a moment where we see the entire world, our entire lives, with absolute clarity. If you have a mathematical mind like myself, then the best I can relate it to is a feeling of solving the hardest mathematical equation of your life and all the variables making perfect sense. The purpose that these people play in the experience of humanity is intentional and needed for this ultimate goal. We just are unable to understand or see it for what it is.

CHAPTER 2

Who am I?

Now that I have given away the surprise ending of our journey together, let us go back to that initial gut feeling of needing to know, "Who am I?" To be honest, I struggled to even get to that question. For years I felt like something was "off" in my life. I could not quite place what was causing this weird feeling in my gut, this feeling that something was missing, that I didn't have all the pieces to the puzzle of my life. So I did what (I think) most people do: I ignored it. I not only ignored it, I piled a whole lot of "busy" on top of it so that that feeling wouldn't rear its ugly head and make me think too hard about it.

You know what I mean by "busy"? I would pack every second of my waking hours with tasks to complete. And if I wasn't physically doing a task, I directed my mind to only think about how to organize my lists of tasks or contemplate the steps to completing a task or solving a problem. Because as long as I kept busy, I didn't have to feel, I didn't have to dig into what was missing inside of me. The messed-up part of this entire paradigm is that I was not conscious of what I was doing. I was not consciously trying not to feel. In fact, I thought I *was* feeling! I thought that I was experiencing all the normal emotions of life. I knew I was certainly feeling all the stress, exhaustion, and anxiety.

I had done everything that I had been taught was how you "made it" and became successful. I had gotten good enough grades to get me into a college. I chose the hardest major I could, computer engineering, and got my master's in network security and engineering management in five years. I was told that the harder that I worked, the more I would reap the rewards. I went on to find a job and worked hard at that. I climbed the corporate ladder. As I did, I found a partner, my husband, and created a family.

For years, the building of my life and the world around me was enough to keep me distracted. I was busy, and I was seeing the things I was told were going to make me happy fall nicely into place. But the truth was that things were not perfect. Under the layers of the perfect family and successful career, I was depressed, exhausted, and suffering from extreme anxiety. It seemed that no matter how I tried to solve those underlying issues, nothing seemed to work. In fact, the more years that went by, the more I found that the issues were getting worse.

It made no sense to me. I had everything that I wanted in my life. I had everything I should have needed to be happy and joyful at my fingertips. Why couldn't I engage in the life that I had spent so many years creating for myself? Why couldn't I relax and enjoy the fruits of all of my labor?

Finally, after years of medicating myself and continually beating myself up over my own shortcomings, that voice that lives inside of me found *its* voice. Somehow, through all of the ways that I had been shutting it down and covering it up, it got through to me. That voice broke through the layers of busyness that I had piled on it, the exhaustion that I had embraced, the numbing I created for myself through focusing on collecting external things.

That voice inside of me broke through the clutter of my life. After years of ignoring my gut, I decided to listen to it. In my naïveté I thought finally dealing with the whispers that I had been hearing would be a simple task that I had just put off for too long. I thought that figuring out exactly who I am was like writing a description of a product. I thought that it was simply a matter of spending some time thinking about myself and that the answers would just be there. That the real problem was that I hadn't ever taken the time to think about it and, when I did, the answer would be so obvious. I thought it was a binomial yes/no answer that I was looking for.

When the answer didn't come in those first few hours of thinking about it, I felt even more empty than I had when I was ignoring that feeling. Facing the emotion that I had been carrying with me and ignoring for years was scary. Facing those emotions and the reality of the situation was what I had been avoiding for my entire adult existence. I had no idea what I had gotten myself into and I really did not have the tools to support the growth that would come. The reality was that I had to really feel the emotions that were in my body instead of pushing them away and ignoring them. My emotions and inner knowledge were so locked up that there was no way for me to untangle them in a single weekend, week, month, or even year.

How could I have lived my entire life, nearly thirty-five years, so unaware of what was happening inside of me? How could I unconsciously repress knowing who I was? At this point, all of the questions flooded in. "When did I forget who I was? How do you forget who you are? Wait, had I ever known?" You can imagine the spiral of questions that you can end up in at this point.

And mine only continued. "Did I know who I was when I was a child, playing in the woods, running around in nature?" No, sadly, I don't think I knew who I was even then. Maybe that's the reason why I always felt there was something missing or that I was so different from everyone around me. No, it wasn't that I was so different, I was just very lost and struggling to find solid footing without a strong understanding of who I was. I don't know if other children have a strong sense of who they are, but it felt like they did.

After months of trying to figure out this feeling in my gut, I realized that I was absolutely sure I could not remember the last time I had known who I was. That realization drove me to finally focus and figure it out. I had the drive and commitment. I was, and still am, after all, a do-er who "gets shit done," as my sister would say. But where does one start to answer a question like this? How do other people figure out who they are? As I looked around me at my friends and loved ones, they seemed to know exactly who they were. It seemed to come effortlessly to them. In fact, I asked my friends, I asked my husband, and yes, yes, they all told me they knew exactly who they were. Was I the only one who didn't know who I was?

The problem I faced was that when I answered those same questions for myself, I knew that the answers, the things that I maybe once believed myself to be, no longer resonated. They weren't truly the core of who I am. It is a tricky thing that happens, how when we start to look around at the people we know and love, we see the masks that they put on for the public. It makes us believe that they know exactly who they are and are in touch with it. But the truth is that when other people looked at me, they would have said the same thing. They would have said that I was x, y, and z, that I had my life together. They would have said that they would love it if they could have a life like (insert a tiny sliver of my life here).

Sure, I was able to describe many traits about myself—I am a hard worker, I am loyal, I am caring, I am many things. But as I made those lists of descriptive words, I knew that there was something deeper at my core. I just couldn't find my way; I wasn't able to get there and see it. That thing that we are all searching for, it's invisible. The only way to know if you have it is a deep knowing inside, a feeling. There isn't a way to look at someone and know if they have it or not. Even with the friends I took my own inventory of, I still to this day don't know how well-connected they are to their inner knowing.

My whole life, I had always thought of myself as fairly nerdy. Just nerdy enough to be socially awkward but not smart enough to really hang with the true intellects. I spent my career leveraging the preconceived notions about my gender (my being a woman in my field was a surprise to many when I started), my age (for much of my career, I was significantly younger than my peers), and my decent-enough looks to constantly surprise people. I threw in a dash of that hard-work mentality from my upbringing and the ability to communicate just a bit better than my smarter and more nerdy counterparts, and voila! A career was born. I had simply held on to my ability to do my job as my entire identity. As long as I was getting external praise and climbing the corporate ladder, I felt I must be doing things right in my life, I must be succeeding. And if I was succeeding then happiness, I was led to believe, would surely follow.

The reality was that I had to look at myself and decide if who I was, who I was *at that exact moment in my life*, was really made up of just those basic descriptors: my job title, wife, mother. Maybe I could have settled on describing myself as my job title or even one step removed, and called myself a career-woman. A woman with ambition and drive isn't so bad of a thing to be, is it? The problem was that that feeling deep in my gut was telling me that there was more to life than that. It was telling me that there was more out there for me, if only I took the time to look for it. Couple that nagging feeling that I simply was not able to escape with the lack of joy I was finding in my career, and an inner drive to constantly grow and you have the perfect recipe for self-growth. For the first time in my life, my job felt unfulfilling and I had a knowing deep down that it was actually pulling me further and further away from my happiness.

So if the way that I was defining myself brought me little to no joy or fulfillment, could that really be the definition of who I was? Could I be satisfied with that? I didn't think so, and, more importantly, I was desperately hoping that there was more depth to me than that.

The funny thing about this journey is that we are all already on it. Whether we know it or not, we are all walking on our divine path. The real question is when are we going to wake up and see where we are. For me, there was not a single moment of clarity, it was a gradual awakening. It was seeing myself as a fish out of water, that I was flailing without a path I could see to take me back to water. It was a knowing that came from somewhere deep inside of me that drove me to look for the path.

I don't know if this is the same for everyone. I don't know if other children have an innate sense of who they are. My guess is that many of us are not aware of who we are, that this forgetting our true essence is part of the human journey. We might think we know who we are, as I did for so long, but there comes a moment where you realize that not everything is what is seems. That the things that you took as truths are actually beliefs that have been passed down generation to generation. Depending on that lineage, each of us has very different beliefs to unravel. We all have different starting points and triggers that bring us back into awareness. Whether you have a single moment that puts you on the path or a building of momentum, like I did, there comes a point where you simply know you must learn more.

CHAPTER 3

The Truth

The first real nugget that I uncovered about who I truly am was that being honest and telling others my truth was a core piece of who I am. This trait of truth-telling was (and still is) both a blessing and a curse. For years, my friends told me that one of the reasons they loved me was because they knew that, if they asked for my opinion, they would get the truth, no sugar-coating. I remember my girlfriends in college checking in with me just to make sure they looked good before they went out for the night, because they knew I would tell them honestly if they didn't. However, on the flip side of that truth is a long trail of hurt feelings and awkward social situations. These often came as strangers, unaware of my propensity toward "truth-telling," would ask me a question, expecting the canned, soft answer, and be shocked at my response when I told them the answers that everyone knew but no one had the guts to tell them. It wasn't that I was intentionally trying to hurt anyone; I simply did not have the awareness that not everyone wants to hear the truth.

I was well aware of the downside of this quality of mine and decided to repackage this "truth-telling" into a more positive quality that I will call "authenticity." I decided, yes, that was what I could lean into, my authentic self. So that is just what I did. I wanted to be the place where women and girls could come to get the cold, hard truth about what life was really like. No sugar-coating of what lies behind the fancy facade put up by the high-powered business women or the ladies who lunch. I was going to reveal the truth of what it really took to be "me," to prepare the women coming up in the world so they wouldn't be surprised when they encountered everything that I had.

I started to lean into authenticity as a means to define myself and started sharing the core of who I was with people; it was both freeing and revealing. I started to slowly remove the layers of illusion that sat between my core self and what others saw. These layers were not lies or even fakeness, but they were parts of myself that I had built up to protect me from getting hurt or being judged. Those layers of illusions were things like the idea that I could have everything on my plate handled; that I could be a perfect wife and mother, while working a high-stress full-time job; that I was happy with the life that I was leading. I was showing people everything I knew about myself.

There is a funny thing about being honest with other people: in order to be honest with others, you have to also be honest with yourself. Those illusions that I had built up to protect myself from others were also shielding me from the awareness of myself. They were blocking insight into what I really needed to be happy and what I could actually take on in a balanced and healthy way.

Why is telling the truth, being vulnerable and honest about who we are, so hard? I started to wonder when exactly it is that we start to cover up who we are and hide it, and why? As I struggled with my own fears of what I might uncover, I started to open up the layers of myself that were on the very outside of that identity onion. My means of sharing my truth with the world was co-founding a blog with two dear friends.

We each had a different approach to what we wanted to share, but it all centered around truth. We named it G.R.I.T., Girls Rise in Truth, a fitting name for a blog written by a girl who relied on her grit to survive life and who was seeking truth.

An amazing thing happened when I shared the truth behind the facade of who I was showing the world: people started to connect with me at the vibration of what I was sharing with them. The more honest and authentic I was with the people around me, the more honest and authentic they were able to be with me. It was as if I was giving them permission to be vulnerable and open up. I was sending the signal that my armor was down so they could lower theirs as well.

It makes sense when you think about it. When you share bits and pieces of yourself, or you share what you think other people want to see, then their only option is to connect to you in a broken and fragmented way. Or, worse yet, when you only offer an illusion to the outside world, then people are only able to connect with an illusion of who you are. Those broken, fragmented, and illusive connections come back to you and that's exactly how you feel—broken and fragmented. Those bonds don't feel solid, because they are not based on a whole or authentic you.

I had been living in a world where I felt like I could only share a part of me, just bits and pieces that I knew people would like and respect. It was a world that I had created for myself based on the rules of society and success that I had picked up on. And at really low points in my life, I would put on my armor, my mask, and become the woman I was supposed to be based on these rules that I had created for myself. I became the woman who I had told the world I was. With my armor and mask securely in place, I would go out and conquer the material and business world, and at night I would come back exhausted from holding all of the protective armor in place.

I thought that conquering the business world and embodying superwoman would make me feel alive and powerful. But those connections and relationships and that power all felt hollow. I had created and was living an illusion; the identity and feeling that I was grasping for and so desperately needed to feel whole had disappeared long ago. My entire life felt like an illusion, an illusion that I created because early on I was not true to myself. And the longer that I continued to support that particular illusion, the stronger that illusion became. My connection to my self became weaker and weaker. I lacked the confidence that I could be successful and, ultimately, that I could be loved for just being me.

The dangerous thing about the mirage that so many of us create is that it sets an example for those following in our footsteps, for our sons and daughters, for the people we mentor, for the people who only see the glamour from the outside. It sets the example that, in order to reach the top, you have to do and be that same false thing. That the cost of success is losing a part of yourself or, at the very least, hiding a part of yourself so you can pretend to be made up completely of what is truly only a tiny sliver of yourself. We highlight the parts of ourselves that we think are desirable, while hiding other parts. And this, my friend, is how I found myself broken and disconnected from who I truly was.

My original goal was to be honest with myself and with the people who I interacted with daily, to show them more than the illusion. What I found was that when I peeled back the layers of illusion and broke down the facade, I found my purpose.

THE TRUTH

CHAPTER 4

Finding Purpose

Finding purpose is tangential to discovering who you are. I think of purpose as icing on the cake of your identity. Finding your purpose can sometimes be more accessible to discover because it is an outward expression of yourself. For me, finding my purpose was a key that unlocked an outer door that gave entrance into a new world that I was able to navigate within to truly find myself.

Ironically, I had found my purpose years before—I just didn't remember it. I had somehow forgotten this golden key to my life. It was like the Universe handed it to me and I looked at it and thought, *That's neat, maybe I'll look at that later, when I have more time.* If I could roll my eyes at my past self, I would right now. It is so obvious to the present me that I was simply "too busy" and caught up in the hustle of life to really appreciate the gift that had been dropped in my lap.

Several years before, I had been suffering from pretty intense bouts of anxiety. I had been on anti-anxiety medication for years, but now it just didn't feel like anything could relieve the tension I felt. I had found a lovely therapist who specialized in anxiety, and I thought that adding therapy into the mix would help alleviate the grip anxiety had on me.

After months of sessions working through specific sources of the anxieties that I experienced, my therapist stopped our normal routine and asked me the simplest of questions: "What is your purpose in life?" I am pretty sure that I looked at her in horror and terror. Not the "Oh, I haven't thought about that" look, but a "Oh, no! I am not prepared to answer this in any sort of way" look. I don't think I even knew how to start to answer the question! In fact, I believe I asked her to clarify the question for me so I could try to figure out what it was exactly that I was supposed to answer.

I don't think we got to an answer in that session. And, in complete avoidance, I spent a lot of time that year digging through the causes of my anxiety to understand why I felt the overwhelming need to control each detail, to understand why I would obsess over the ways in which a scenario might go wrong. I realize now, in the clarity that comes with hindsight, that the sheer panic I felt when she initially asked the question about my life purpose was not because I didn't know the purpose of my life. The panic that I felt in that moment was driven by the fact that I was scared of who I believed myself to be. And that feeling of panic was compounded with intense shame.

Thinking back as far as I can, even in my earliest childhood memories, I only ever remember thinking that I was put in this world to do stuff, to be a builder. I thought that my purpose was to be a worker bee. I had hope that I was not just a worker bee who toils and toils, but a worker bee who would work so hard that one day I would break free of the shackles of my lowly position and have a hive of my own. (We are going to just ignore the fact that, as far as I know, I don't think worker bees turn into queen bees in real beehives!) The truth was that I had felt pressure to be that worker bee, to be the reliable do-er so I could reach my destiny. And I felt guilty about that ambition. My. Whole. Life. That's how long I had felt that way.

It is a hard thing to come face to face with the belief that your purpose in life is to work hard, that the value you add to the people around you only comes from "putting in the work," and that there is nothing more valuable for you to add.

It's silly, really. It was a paradox of thinking. Why should I feel bad for wanting financial stability when, at the same time, I was willing to work myself to death to obtain it? Yet again, when viewing all of it from where I sit today, it is so clear that I was misguided. The anxiety and guilt came from this false belief that my purpose, and thus my self-worth, were tied to the amount that I worked and what I produced.

Yes, it is true that I want to live comfortably, and it will always be something that I put some of my energy toward. I want my family to live in comfort too, with a roof over their heads and enough food to eat. But digging into my purpose in life helped me see that I had missed out on living while I chased the material dreams. That the work that I was doing and the things that I was creating were hollow, missing the soul or spirit of something bigger.

After months of avoiding doing the hard work of looking within myself and instead working through the many other aspects of whatever it was that was happening in my life at the time, I sat in yet another therapy session, where my wonderful therapist asked me if I had thought about what my purpose was. And it just came to me, without panic or fear, without dread or shame. My purpose was something that I had known for nearly all of my life. I had just buried the knowledge deep inside myself because, somewhere along the way to growing up, I had taken on the belief that this purpose made me weak, that this thing that I was meant to do would make me too vulnerable to survive in the harsh world that I had lived in, that I needed to create and build armor to protect this essence to survive. The cascade of that sort of belief is vast, like a snowball rolling downhill and out of control. I can now see how the smallest of insecurities or snippets of self-doubt I might have felt as a child took off like a runaway train. I can see the implications of believing that I needed to hide my true purpose and instead build armor to protect myself until I reached success. This was a monumental pivot.

I can imagine how, as a young child growing up (in a much different time than today) in a non-traditional home with a Korean immigrant mother and white father, that I started to believe that I had to hide who I was. When I looked around, there were no other kids who looked like me, and there were no other families who ate the "weird" food that we ate. I have a distinct memory of going to school with a lunchbox full of all of my favorite things from home, all of my favorite Korean dishes. I remember the embarrassment that I felt as all the kids made fun of me that day, as they told me that the food I was eating was gross and that I was weird.

It is no wonder that I hid who I was, or tried to make myself appear more and more "white" and my home life more and more "normal." It is no wonder that my self-worth started to dwindle as I saw myself through the eyes of my schoolmates. I can see my confidence and exuberance for life dim as I began to suppress my spirit from being expressed. I believe that our self-worth and self-confidence are tied to knowing who and what we are, and sharing that with the world is what feeds our life force and energy.

You might be wondering what this hideous purpose that I have in life is, that I felt like I had to hide it away. Well, my purpose is very simple. I have been blessed with this life to support and inspire others, to help people—and myself—find their way back to their truest and best selves. I am sure there are parts of this purpose that will manifest in bigger ways, such as this book. But for most of my life (when I have been aware of and in touch with my divine purpose), I have believed that this influence that I have on people comes mostly in the smallest of forms, like smiling at strangers or offering kind words when someone is down. I have believed, and still to this day believe, that my most impactful actions are ones that I will never know about. They are the actions that I take that spark transformations that I never get to actually witness.

I don't know what transpired in my childhood mind that led me to believe that my purpose wasn't good enough or strong enough for the world I lived in. There was no one instant that I can remember that changed the course of my life into the detour that I took. But I do hold deep gratitude for the child who I was and the journey through life that I took to get to this place now. I trust and know deeply that I needed to take that path, to experience the detour so I could relate and offer a deeper compassion to the people who I help today. I am also grateful for those therapy sessions. They restarted me on the journey to finding myself once again.

CHAPTER 5

The Detours of Life

If my life were a fairytale or even a made-for-TV movie, the next scene would be me living my life's purpose, happy and blissed out, with all the success in the world. But the reality is that I am not living a fairytale, nor a movie. I am living our shared human experience, meaning that, while I had grasped my purpose in life, it didn't actually make it very deep into my body. It's like I was given this key to my happiness on a piece of paper and said, "Thanks, I'll just read that later."

My life moved on in much the same way that it had up until that point. I continued in my same job, frantically packing my life full of things to do, avoiding all of the emotion and depth within me. I did all this while my anxiety continued to increase. I unconsciously avoided any break in life that would force me to take a deeper look at what was really going on inside of me. I continued like that for years, in what I like to call "a highly functioning ball of anxiety." I'm sure there is a more technical or medically correct term for that, but I was essentially locked up in pure anxiety unless I was in front of a client or my staff. On the outside, I continue to be the picture of success and happiness, but on the inside there was always a knowing that something was missing and something was very wrong. My entire chest felt tight and locked up, like I could barely move unless I forced myself to.

As my career continued to progress, I found myself spending less and less time at home. More and more of my responsibilities required me to be the face of my team, to lift people up and reassure both our staff and clients. All of this meant I needed to be in front of people constantly. My kids were growing up, they were all out of the youngest ages when they still wanted to cling, and I mistakenly thought that the older they were, the less they would need me. The reality is that the older they are, the more they know and feel your absence. As they age, they simply have more awareness of how connected (or disconnected) you are from the conversations and activities that they are asking you to participate in.

Then one day a perfect storm happened. Again, I attribute this convergence of events to the divine plan or, more accurately, to a divine intervention. It had been a particularly hard few weeks of travel, I had been in multiple cities back-to-back, and I felt like I had barely been home. Two of my three kids happened to say something to me as I prepared and packed for yet another trip. They were clearly calling me out for how much of their lives I was missing. And while I placated them with false hopes and promises that I would be home more in the future, something about their words struck me. Those words stuck and dug themselves down deep within me, as only truth can do.

During this same time, I had a particularly persistent recruiter reach out to me. She had been calling and emailing for months. Usually a polite "no, thank you" did the trick with recruiters, but this woman finally convinced me to just take a single call with the hiring manager for the role she wanted me to consider. The brand she worked for was well-respected and globally known. Together, the recruiter and hiring manager did a great job of selling me on the dream of making an impact on a world-famous brand, all while getting to eat dinner with my kids every night.

I still wasn't completely convinced though. I had spent the last fifteen years of my life and career at the same company, building relationships and climbing the ranks. The intense loyalty of my Scorpio sign was coming into play and I just couldn't convince myself to abandon the company and team I thought of as family. Yet, as fate would have it, that next trip that I was getting ready for was an executive offsite in Costa Rica. (Yes, I know, even now I think to myself in a sarcastic tone, *Poor you, you were flying all over the world to amazing locations to work.* Even today, it is easy to see the allure of the life that I was giving off the illusion that I had.)

I had thought that this trip was just what I needed to realign with my organization and reconnect with what inspired me to show up each day. In my mind, I had thought that some time strategizing with my counterparts and eating some good meals in a tropical location would rejuvenate me. Unfortunately, the trip did nothing of the sort. While we were in the beautiful tropics, just steps away from the sand and salty sea, we were stuck in meetings. Yes, we were in a beautiful location, but we were stuck inside rooms with too many hot bodies, all of us looking out the windows yearning for even a few minutes to break and enjoy the beauty around us. Instead of feeling connected and rejuvenated, the hours upon hours of meetings left the entire team exhausted and uninspired.

The final nail in the coffin was when the new CEO stood up and, as part of his pep talk, announced that we should all plan to be on more flights in the coming year. He believed that what the company needed to get us to the "next level" was more face time with the company's leaders—all of us. I think I may have blacked out for just a millisecond. Had I heard that correctly? He wanted us to be on more flights? Visiting more cities? I could not imagine being away from home more than I already was. I wasn't sure it was even possible!

And that was the end of that. Yes, it took me weeks to finish negotiating the details of my transition with both sides, but ultimately I think the decision was made in the instant those words left the CEO's mouth.

And then I was off, on to a new adventure with hopes and dreams of the perfect life ahead. I had committed to myself and my husband that I would take this new job on and give it a year before making any judgments. My husband had just switched jobs as well, and I knew from that experience that you had to take some time for the new routine and culture to settle in. I knew how hard it would be to transition into a new role and new organization after so many years of building my team at one company. I thought that, if I just gave myself time to build those types of relationships and prove my value, I would find my footing and thrive.

I am thankful that I made that commitment. As I walked into my new office on that first day, my entire body screamed at me to run. You know the scenes in movies when a character walks into a room and you know they are about to be killed? The premonition that the character has and that's clear to the viewers, but the character ignores it? That was the feeling I had and that I, too, promptly ignored. Part of me wishes that I had listened to myself, that I was strong enough or knowledgeable enough to make the decision to walk away sooner. But the other part of me is extremely grateful for the wisdom that I learned throughout that year.

That first day was dreadful. The people all looked so sad working at their desks, too lost in their own depressed worlds to welcome a new person onto the team. No one seemed to know who I was or why I was there, much less where I was to sit or how I was going to get a computer. The first few months that followed were painful. I went from highly sought after and respected within my previous organization and by our clients to barely worthy of a weekly check-in with my new boss. It was a good lesson in humility, to say the least. It also taught me that I still had some of my scrappiness left in me from when I had to climb the ranks the first time around. I found ways into that organization, ways to add value and yet again prove my worth.

As the months wore on, I found my footing and thought that maybe that feeling I had had that first day was wrong. Maybe I had been right to ignore it. I had carved out my world and was starting to get noticed and respected. But the thing about finding that success was that I had given up even more in my personal life to achieve it. That dream of eating dinner with my kids every night? I never came close to being able to do that. Even though I was no longer jumping on flights all over the country, I was somehow home even less. I was missing even more of my kids' lives. At least in my previous role I had had some flexibility when I was home. I could schedule a break to run and volunteer at school or show up for a holiday party. Now I was gone before they woke for school and was getting home long after they had eaten dinner and moved on to their nightly homework or other activities. And while they had the energy to engage with me at that point in the day, I was completely wrung out and exhausted.

I found myself in a worse predicament that I had been in before. Not only was I overworked and completely burned out, I also no longer had the strong supportive network that I had had at my previous company. And, as happens when you find yourself in dark times, the Universe stepped in, yet again, to illuminate my way.

The first little nudge I got was about six months before I actually made a change. I started getting a very clear feeling that I needed to put my marriage first, and that if I didn't do that soon that I would lose it. There wasn't a specific outward indicator that my marriage was in trouble; it was cruising along as it had been for years. But deep inside I knew that it was now or never to bring us back together, back into connection with each other. So I made a commitment to myself that I would start to prioritize my marriage. I had no idea how that would happen given our demanding careers and work schedules, but I committed nonetheless.

A month or two after this point, and likely because I had taken little to no action to move in the direction of my divine path, my boss, who had been unavailable and unaccounted for at best, showed back up in my life in a big way. Apparently, that "success" that I had been feeling at work? She had been feeling it too... just not in the way that I had hoped. Instead of being excited or proud of the work that I had done for our group, she was quite angry that I had been attending meetings with executives above what she called "my pay grade." I think the final blow to our quasi-working relationship was when she found out that I was being invited to senior-level meetings and that she was being intentionally left out. The repercussions of this were swift and direct, landing a debilitating blow to my self-worth and my ability to properly function in my role at work.

My boss essentially directed that I could no longer meet with or communicate with anyone who held a title that was above my own. I was to report to her if anyone at a level above mine emailed or contacted me, and all correspondence was to go through her. I will tell you that I have done my work on this. I have dug deep and looked at myself. And while I am sure there is another part to this sordid tale, I can say that I did my due diligence to understand what misstep I might have taken with others in the organization at the time and was unable to find one. What I am very clear on is that I needed a sign, a signal, as strong as this one to force me onto my divine path. I needed a sign that cut me to the core of who I was and what I held in the highest esteem. I needed something that made me question my values, what truth really was. And this was it.

At the time I was angry, frustrated, and probably more than a little bitter. The hopes and dreams I had had about where I thought I would be when I took that big leap of faith never panned out. The reality of the detour was cold and hard. Yet, when I look back on my own journey, I hold an immense amount of gratitude for this part of my life. If I had not had the courage to leave my previous company after fifteen years to take on this opportunity, I don't know that I would have ever left. I might even still be there today, far away from my truth that I get to experience and live every day.

I learned so much during my time at that new company. I learned about the power and importance of culture in an organization and group setting and about the role that leadership plays in influencing masses of people, and I found my own strength and the importance of my beliefs on how we treat one another. That work experience pushed me so far outside of the bounds of my comfort that I was forced to reckon with who I wanted to be and what I was willing to give up in order to obtain it. Those detours in life are what set us up for the miracles we get to experience next.

I have a deep appreciation for the detours that I have experienced in my own journey. It is now clear to me that the experience and knowledge I gained in each of the twists and turns that I took in life support how

I help people today. Without the time I spent working with executives at so many Fortune 500 companies, I would not be able to relate to the clients that I support today. I had to take that path to gain awareness and empathy for the people who are experiencing the same things that I did. Those chapters of my life that I spent lost and confused allow me to support the transformation of others who are just like me.

CHAPTER 6

Shamanic Intervention

As you will come to find out, or possibly have already discovered, the Universe gives you just what you need, right when you need it. It is like the scene from Disney's *Onward*, when the main character, Ian Lightfoot, must cross the trust bridge. Ian must conjure the "invisible bridge spell" to cross over the deep canyon, as the bridge has fallen out. In this scene, you learn that the secret to the spell is that Ian must believe that the next step of the bridge will be there when he puts his foot down. The moment he questions if the bridge will be there, the spell will break and he will fall to his doom. But as long as he believes, the spell works and he can cross to the other side safely.

It is hard to create that belief, that trust, in a specific moment when you need it most. But when you are on the other side looking back, it is much easier to see that the steps were laid out for you as you moved forward. It is with this perspective, looking back at my own journey, that I am able to see Spirit, the Universe, laying down my steps as I walked forward on my path.

And, as the Universe does, she offered me the opportunity to meet with a shamanic healer at just the exact moment when I could take in such an offer and truly utilize the gift. This opportunity fell in my lap as a friend of a friend of a friend connected me to this person that would play such a pivotal in my life. To be honest, I had no idea what I was getting myself into at the time. As a reminder, when I took this meeting I was still deep in my conditioned mind that success would come from hard work (and nothing else), I was suffering from anxiety (though I had reduced my medication significantly), and I was simply exhausted from keeping myself too busy to feel.

There is simply no way to have foreseen the shift this first meeting would cause in the trajectory of the rest of my life. However, I was excited to talk to this teacher. I had this feeling, a knowing deep down in the center of my stomach, that this was something that I had to do. The feeling wasn't like an obligation, but it was a feeling of knowing that, after this first meeting, I would never be the same. For someone who was so out of touch with herself, I feel like this was my spirit giving me one last kick to get me back on my truest path.

Once I had made the decision to meet this great teacher, I felt an urgency to make it happen. So after that first meeting with them, we decided that I would attend ceremony in just a few short weeks. I was to prepare for the ceremony by spending time in nature, cleaning up my diet, cutting out any alcohol, getting completely off my medication, and meditating on my intentions.

Let me be perfectly clear here. I could spend time in nature, even though I was so caught up in my head that I wasn't really seeing it. I could follow the rules set forth on diet, drinking, and my anxiety medication. But these intentions that I was to create and meditate on? Those I had no idea how to even approach. I simply was not equipped in my psyche to know how to do this. I harken back to trying to figure out my life's purpose and the task being so beyond my realm of knowledge that I just couldn't do it. The morning of the ceremony, I was a nervous ball of energy, running around the house doing whatever it was I could find and make up to distract myself. My husband stopped me and gently asked if he could help me put some pictures together for me to take to the ceremony. I thought, *Sure, why not?* It might be comforting to have some pictures of the people I love most close to me during this experience. And, with the gentlest of reminders, he asked what intentions he should add to the miniature poster he was creating for me. Without a second thought, I said, "Lightness in my soul."

That was the first time I can remember having a divinely channeled experience. I didn't know that was what it was at the time, but I can assure you now that that is what it was. I was even confused at the time as to what had just happened when he asked if I was sure that was what I wanted on my poster. My response was "yes" and, "I don't know why I said that, but it's what has to go on there." I didn't even know what it meant, much less why I was asking for it to be on the poster!

As the afternoon sun dipped down into a gorgeous red and orange sunset, I climbed the stairs to the front door of this fairly normal house in the suburbs. My heart was beating out of my body. I was nervous, I was sweating profusely, and I was all alone. It felt like this was the first time I was really stepping out of my comfort zone and doing something for myself and by myself. As I entered the split-level, I looked up the stairs and made eye contact with a beautiful wise woman. I could feel her wisdom and love radiating off of her. She was a lovely Korean woman, just about my mother's age, and radiated motherly love and acceptance. I went to make my introduction and it became clear that we did not speak the same language—she did not speak English.

I continued to make my way into the space of ceremony and was directed to my place to sit. The others had been there for the previous two evenings and were all completely settled into their own spaces; I was the only newcomer to the evening's experience.

We were called to gather around the altar as the shamanic priestess guided us through the opening of the ceremony. As the time came to share our intentions with the group, the motherly Korean woman began, with her daughter there to interpret for us. I think I blacked out; I don't remember what she shared, nor do I remember what the others shared. I just remember the feeling that my intention was shallow and maybe a little selfish. I was consumed with the feeling of being unprepared and unworthy of such an experience. While the others shared intentions of world peace, unified love, and a vast number of other intentions for the greater good of the world, my intention was solely about me. It was to bring lightness to my soul. I didn't even know what that meant, much less how that could help anyone beyond myself. With a bit of shame, I quietly made my way back to my place in the circle and the ceremony continued.

I sat there meditating, something that I had never been good at to begin with, and I wondered what in the world I was doing there. I sensed that the rest of the people in the room seemed to be operating on a different level than me and I honestly could not even imagine myself getting there. I didn't even know where "there" was! So, with that thought on my mind, I settled in for what I thought was going to be a long, slow night of watching from the outside with little understanding of what was really happening. But, just as I settled into this acceptance of what was to come, the woman directly across from me (the Korean woman) started to cry. And when I say she started to cry, she really started to cry, which then turned into what can only be described as wailing. The sound reverberated through my body and I felt my body starting to respond in much the same way I had responded to any discomfort my entire life: I got annoyed and then started to get angry. Who was this woman to cry this loudly? And how long was this going to last? Was the entire group to endure this sound for the entire night? How dare she interrupt the sacredness of the ceremony with these sounds?

The second those thoughts passed through my mind, I was given the answer. "No, you don't have any idea what is happening. She is crying for you. She is crying because you are unable to." Holy sh!t! This woman, sitting across from me in this circle, was literally crying for me! How was that possible? And was I that broken that I couldn't even cry for myself? (The answer to that is yes, I was "that broken" that I could not even cry for myself.)

As that realization dawned on me, I felt the first tears fall down my face. The moment played out over and over in my head. I had been, just seconds ago, completely at my wits' end with a woman who was literally wailing for me because I was unable to do it for myself. Just how selfish and egotistical was I? How blind was I to not be able to see someone so selflessly helping me? How much had I missed or gotten wrong in the rest of my life? I processed all of that (and the mind-blowing fact that someone can literally cry for another person to help release their emotions) until it felt like there were no more tears left to give, like I had cried out years of repressed sadness. It was time to rest.

I laid my head down and covered my eyes. I felt like I had done my work for the night; what more could happen after another person had purged emotion for you? Except I wasn't done. I was nowhere near done with the work of the evening. I laid down, closed my eyes to rest, and drifted off into a dreamlike state. I was lying asleep on a makeshift bed of blankets and a few pillows, but as I drifted into this alternate mind state, the bed that I was lying on, while comfortable, turned into a bed made of wood. The wood was almost like driftwood, or round poles that had been strung together. As I laid there drifting further into the dream state, I felt the bed lift from the ground. Now, floating just above the ground, I wondered if I should open my eyes, just to check and make sure I was okay. I was wrestling with my grip on reality. I wasn't sure what was real or what was happening to me. But, for whatever reason, at that moment I thought to myself, *No, you're not that far off the ground, you'll be fine*, and simply accepted the situation I found myself in. So, floating just above the ground, as I laid on that wood pallet made of poles, I started to move. I moved out of the room, through ancient doors, and out onto the streets of what I would describe as the ancient Middle East. In all honesty, it felt a lot like floating out into the scene from *Aladdin* when they are in the market stealing the food. It felt both very real and also contrived, like I was on a movie set. As I pondered what exactly was happening, I continued to float through the market until another realization dawned on me.

I was dead. Wait, what?!? *I'm dead. How could this be?* I had just been alive, thinking about how I could have been transported to this other place while simply lying on a few blankets in a room. But no, this wooden bed that I thought that I was asleep on was actually a funeral pyre. The lovely tour through the market that I had just experienced was the funeral procession to my burning. And yet, through all of this revelation and understanding, there was no part of me that felt fear. Confusion, sure, there was a lot of it. But there was some comfort too. I knew I had died, but I also knew that part of me needed to die and the rest of me was perfectly safe back in the room where we were holding the ceremony.

In that cocoon of safety, I was immediately transported back to the ceremony. I sat up and took in my surroundings, finding my footing and reality. I thought to myself, *What in the world just happened? Had I fallen asleep? Was that a dream?* I don't think I'll ever really know what happened. Maybe it is better to not know or understand all the inner workings of how healing happens. What is important is that I know that a part of me died in that experience; a part that needed to be shed and released, allowing the new, fresh me to emerge.

The rest of the ceremony was spent catching up with the foreshadowing of the prophecy of that dreamlike state. The woman across from me, who I now know to be from a long line of great Mongolian shamans, continued to work with me throughout the night. The things that I experienced were beyond my wildest imagination or any semblance of what I thought reality was. She worked with me to pull demons that I had been carrying with me since childhood out of my body. In a very literal sense I felt these demons being purged from my body. They took shape as black dragons made up of tiny geometric shapes and angles, but were in the form of smoke or looked like liquid when it is dropped into another liquid and you can see them mix. They were perfectly shaped and also fluid to the environment they were in. Each dragon that came from my body represented repressed emotion. The first ones that were purged made logical sense; they were the most painful and likely the ones that were keeping me captive in my own body. They were the pain from a sexual assault at the age of eleven and then again as a teen, the burden of abuse endured as a child, the shame from being and feeling "different" than the white kids at school. Eventually, the logic and tangible attachment to specific incidents or feelings faded, giving way to the release of nearly every last drop of darkness that

I had been carrying. The only thing left was the open space in me. I felt a lightness I had never experienced before. I felt like I had lost weight in the night, like the heavy burdens that I had carried were simply gone. I felt full of only light; the darkness was gone.

At the end of the night, I barely knew what to make of my experience. It would take me months and maybe even years to completely unravel what exactly had happened that night. What I was certain of was that I was forever changed. I knew it deep in my heart. I could never go back to "before." There simply wasn't a path I would walk or a possibility that I was going to let those dragons, those demons, that darkness back in.

CHAPTER 7

Committing to Myself

I left that night wondering why everyone in the world hadn't taken the leap and done something like this. I was full of love, with light radiating off of me. I knew this was how we were all meant to feel, it was how we were built, to operate at this higher frequency. If everyone could feel the way that I felt, the entire world would be different. I knew something profound had been unlocked in me. Something was released from deep in my soul that night. It was something that I had carried with me my entire life, possibly from a past lifetime or lifetimes. I had never felt so light—I literally felt as if I had lost five or ten pounds, and had a new sense of light filling me. My intention was for lightness in my soul and that is exactly what I got. And yet I had no way of knowing just what it was that I was asking for as I entered into that space.

I had had the foresight to take the recommendation of the guide to take that next day off from work. I spent the day basking in the sun, literally. I laid out on our back deck in the brisk Pacific Northwest sun. It wasn't particularly warm that day, but I could feel each ray of light entering my body and replenishing something deep inside of me where I had been essentially empty. This place was hidden beneath the layers and layers of protection that I had built. It was the dragons that had been protecting it, protecting me.

To be honest, I don't remember when I realized what those dragons really were or what their purpose was in my life, but I know now exactly what they are. Those beautifully haunting black geometric dragons are the guardians of the divine realm. They were created from trauma and fear (I still do not know if they are from this lifetime alone or if I was carrying them over from past lives lived). And, contrary to my initial belief that they were demons or something nefarious that I had to get out, they were beautiful spirits that had been protecting me. They were the things allowing me to function at such a high level without truly having to face the truth of who and what

I was. So it is with gratitude and awe that I remember the blessing of having held them in my body, and it is with gratitude and awe that I live my life born a new woman strong enough to shine my inner light.

It was this new woman who walked back into work the next day. You may think, as I did, that I could walk back into work as this new woman, with a new lease on life, and like in any good fairytale go on to change the world. I could be the one to fill everyone's heart with love and compassion for one another. Well, let me tell you, that is not what that first day was like. No, not at all. Imagine a baby deer, barely able to walk, completely disoriented and caught in headlights. That is a more accurate picture of what I felt like, though I'm sure I held it together better than that on the outside—or I hope that I did! But what became immediately clear was that it was going to be very difficult for this new woman to thrive in the construct that I had been living in.

The world that I had left just three days ago was now completely misaligned with the person who I knew myself to be. I had been thrown out of the matrix, swallowed the red pill, and the reality that was revealed to me could not be forgotten. It had changed the very core of my belief system and who I knew myself to be. I didn't know how I was going to align this new knowledge with the construct and reality of what was going on around me. Deep down I knew I had changed too much and I simply couldn't stay. To my great luck— or, more accurately, by Divine plan—I only needed to navigate and survive a week or two before leaving for a preplanned eighteen-day adventure rafting down the Grand Canyon with my family.

The trip was amazing. I stepped into a vortex in time and space, cut off from the outside world, and was completely immersed in nature. It was exactly what I needed. When you are cut off from the outside world of technology and literally a mile down into the Earth's surface, there is no escaping the wonder that Mother Nature truly is. I spent the week in true appreciation and awe of rocks, animals, Mother Earth, and Mother Nature. The moonlight at night was so bright that it often felt as if we were living on a different planet, illuminated by a foreign sun. During the day, the sun burned so bright and hot that the refuge of the icy river water was often welcome. As we embarked on our return to the real world, I felt refreshed, renewed from the connection to nature and the disconnection from the world of societal illusion. I felt like I could be me and approach life with the same drive I had before, just surrounded with a new lightness and energy.

However, not even halfway back to our flights that awaited us, as we came into cell phone coverage, a message came in that my mother had suffered multiple strokes and was in the hospital. She was alive, but the prognosis was unknown. The shock of the news was jarring to this new sense of peace that I had found. I fell right back into the mode of do-er, that safe space where I felt the most protected and where I had lived most of my life. It was not immediate, but I can see now that it was facing the possible loss of my mother and the realization that I was wasting my precious time focused on the things of life rather than the love in life that drove me to quit my job.

I have to pause and acknowledge here just how difficult taking that actual step was, both for myself and for anyone else who is contemplating it. There are infinite layers that one must work through in order to find the courage to take that leap. I was no different. My mother fully recovered from her strokes, which is a miracle in and of itself. I know that her health scare was just what I needed to push me over the edge and find the courage to step onto my path.

I doubt that I would have been able to actually do it without the unwavering support of my husband. He helped me through the moments of panic about everything from the loss of income to the loss of identity to the infinite number of worries about future events that would likely never happen. The choice is difficult and freeing all at once. I understand why so many people stay when we know that the career or job we do brings us little or no joy. Sometimes it is easiest to stay with the thing you know and that feels safe rather than take the leap into the unknown that feels scary.

Another moment of honesty here: I don't know how I actually found the courage to leave. But I did. And, in retrospect, I can see leaving my career as a major stepping-stone on my path, maybe even the *most* pivotal stepping-stone on my direct path back to myself. I see it now as my signal to the Universe and Spirit that I was committed to really doing the work. I was making the commitment to us; I was making the commitment to *me*. That step is what unlocked everything else that has unfolded in my life. I am so grateful for the divine intervention that allowed me to do it.

That decision sparked something inside of me. In leaving the only world that I had ever known, I was left to reassess what I really wanted in my life, what was most important to me, and, more importantly, what I was willing to give up to get those things. Knowing what I wanted out of life was easy, as I'm sure it is for you too. I want love, connection, and probably some level of success. The questions I had to ask myself were, "Am I willing to give up my identity and 'success' in the eyes of work colleagues and outer society? Am I willing to have people who know me only through work or who keep up with me on social media think that maybe I am failing, or worse, going crazy? And, if those people think that, do I think that too?" I had to really assess how many of the thoughts going through my mind were thoughts that I was having about myself and how many of them were truly outside perspectives influencing me.

What I had to realize was that my definition of success was changing (and that that was okay). I shifted from my self-worth being tied to external success, input, and accolades from colleagues to viewing success and my self-worth as internally driven. My view shifted to how good I felt I was doing at raising good humans who would feel fulfilled in their own lives; to having a strong connection with my husband to ensure we were both feeling fulfilled and supported in our marriage; to giving something back to the people I love and care about, to society. Those things can't be measured in my title or in the amount of money I earn. They can't be measured in a single moment. Those are long-term goals and measures of a lifetime. Those are the things that can really only be viewed accurately after I am gone, after I have left my own stamp on the world. I had to have faith that the work that I was putting in would matter and make a difference years down the road, not necessarily today.

✦

CHAPTER 8

Upgrading My Mind, Body, and Soul

I had done it! I had quit my job. Now what?

That first week I settled into a pretty lovely routine; it felt like vacation. I took advantage of all the free time to do the things that I loved to do. I worked out every day, I planned lunch with friends, I was home and excited to make snacks as the kids returned from school. But as the time slowly moved on and the initial excitement of freedom wore off, I panicked. I found myself in a constant track of worry that I had made the wrong decision, that I would never be able to get my career and identity back, that I would simply disappear since I was no longer anything important or special.

In retrospect, I view this time in my journey as both a test of my commitment to finding myself and as a cleansing of the last drops of the old paradigm holding onto me. To cope with the loss of my career identity, I threw myself full-on into mom mode. I decided I could be the most present mom there ever was! I was going to be the best! But there was one small problem with that: my children were now maybe a tad too old to have me all over the details of their lives. I now had a fifth grader (I had a little time left with that one) and a sophomore, and a senior in high school. I might have missed being a supermom by just a few years.

I spent those next several months fighting and weaseling my way into their lives in any way that I could. And, with the rest of my time, I was diving deeper and deeper into my meditation and mindfulness practice. I found myself signing up for workshops and classes on everything from the meaning of crystals, to what the Akashics were and how to access them, to how to develop your intuitive and energy work abilities, to how the brain can rewire itself. I even audited a college course on neurobiology and its ties to psychology. I was a sponge, soaking up all there was to know about how to get better at just being.

Had you asked me just a few months prior if there was a way to upgrade your neural connections, to change the actual connections in your brain, or alter your DNA, I would have looked at you and thought that you were "woo-woo" or "way out there" and maybe a little crazy. Yet just a few short months later, that is exactly what I was experiencing. Through a process of deep meditative states, journeying to the inner worlds, and visits with my new shamanic teacher and guide, I found that my body was slowly being upgraded. Over several months, I had experiences that defied conventional logic and blew many of my beliefs of truth out of the water. I still to this day do not have a clear scientific explanation for what I have experienced.

The beginning of this phase, which I think of as my "bodily upgrade," started with a rewiring of my brain. As I laid in a deep state of meditation, I felt the neuropathways that had been core to my existence up until that point being disconnected and reconnected into new patterns and formations. I have thought of it as wires being unplugged and then re-plugged into different outlets. Imagine the images or movies of the phone operators of old when they were literally connecting and disconnecting the phone lines; it felt a lot like that, but on a micro-level. While this experience could have been scary, there was deep comfort in knowing that all of these physical changes were to allow me to see and feel who I truly am. I came out of that experience with a deep knowing that I had been reprogrammed to only be able to see and feel love. I couldn't quite wrap my mind around how that could be, but at the same time, I knew it to be true.

Just as with the shedding of the layers that surrounded my inner light, which had manifested as dragons to me, I could see the higher and greater good that was coming from this work. There was a clear construct of my future and how to get there. It was clear that I had to "do the work" to shed the armor that I had built and put in place my entire life. Even with the removal of the outer guards, I still had layers and layers of this heavy armor that needed to be removed so the core of my essence, my being and soul, could be set free and shine.

As the weeks passed, I felt myself moving further and further inward. To the outside world, this probably looked a lot like me retreating back into my own physical space, slowly disconnecting from friends and focusing only on family. I found myself sitting in my living room for long periods of time, bouncing back and forth between meditating and consuming more knowledge, with short breaks to engage with my husband and kids. At one point I joked that I was obsessively learning and working on manifesting my future self. (I wasn't too far off the mark.) And, just to be clear, I really had no idea what I was doing. I just knew that the information had my attention and the meditation brought me back into a calmness that I had never experienced before in my life.

Yet it was this next experience that brought my awareness to a larger plan that was at play. The night before I was to attend another shamanic healing ceremony, I had the most vivid dream. It was so clear that it felt as real as sitting here writing this book. In my first ceremony, there was a fairly large detail that was left unresolved. I had found myself floating through the streets atop a pyre. I knew that I had died, but at no point in that journey during that ceremony did I actually catch fire and burn. I remember thinking at the time that it was odd that I would die and be put on an object as specific as a pyre, but not burn, not complete the ceremony. After all, couldn't I have just died and moved into some other form or simply died and had that be it? Why the pyre? Why the ceremony? But with everything else that happened that night, the detail of the forgotten pyre ended up being the last thing on my mind.

But that night, as I was preparing for this next ceremony, the purpose of the pyre was made clear. I had fallen asleep as I normally do, nothing unusual about my preparations for bed. However, about halfway through the night, it felt as if I had awoken (but I was still asleep). I was back on that funeral pyre, moving from the streets of the market down to the riverbank. In many ways I felt at ease; I had been here before. But there was discomfort as well, as I was being moved by people or forces beyond my control or knowledge. The people around me were both strangers and familiar, all at once. The entire situation was confusing and disorienting. Just as I was coming to grips with what was going on around me, I was lit on fire. I could feel the heat move up my body—not in a painful way, just factually I knew the heat was moving up, through, and around me. As I caught fire, they moved me fully onto the river to burn to completion.

So it was with a steady heart, some hard-earned experience from the last time, and this profound experience from the night before that I returned the next night to my next ceremony. I settled into my place amongst the participants. In some ways I found it more difficult to drop in and to do the work this time around. I had expectations and prior experience to lead my mind to what it should be like. But if I know anything now about the way that the Divine works, it is that you should expect the unexpected. Anything that I think I know, Spirit flips on its head, and Spirit always delivers exactly what I need, but not always what I thought that I wanted. It is exactly that false belief in expectation and knowing that posed the challenge to me.

When I was finally able to drop into the experience, I started to touch the edges of the spiritual realm. I found that my body was under a cascade of ribbons made of golden light. It was unlike anything I have ever seen or imagined. These ribbons of light were falling down onto my body and absorbing into my skin. It was as if I was being recharged by a higher energy source. Just as I got comfortable with the feeling of being recharged and rejuvenated, the experience changed. The ribbons seamlessly disappeared and, at that same, these tiny bubbles of light instantly started to emanate from my body. Imagine tiny bubbles the size that you would find in a champagne glass, but these were made of divine light. That is what was floating up from my body. It was almost a celebration or party; it was joy emanating from my body. I had transmuted the divine light that had entered my body into these bubbles of joy.

Just as I was able to take in the wonder and awe of the moment, the feeling in my body shifted yet again. It was as if my body had been paralyzed. I could not move, and panicked for just a moment until I realized that I had turned into a crystal, a human-sized light blue crystal.

I would love to be able to tell you that I stayed calm and felt only love in that moment, but the truth is that it felt like I was encased inside of the crystal. I did not feel at one with it; it felt confining and slightly more claustrophobic than was comfortable for my psyche. But instead of moving toward the panic, as I lay on the floor completely immobilized, I found that I went back to my breath and tapped into my meditation practice.

I knew that I wasn't alone, that eventually someone would notice that I was lying in the same spot, unable to move, and come to help me if I needed it.

Luckily, I did not end up needing someone to come and break me out of that energetic crystal. Instead, I slowly began to become the crystal itself. What started as a singular crystal encasing my entire body slowly changed to crystals that encased each of my limbs, then muscles, then organs, then cells, and ultimately each individual molecule in my body turned into a crystal shape. As I thought back on that experience, it occurred to me that maybe this is what people refer to when they say they have had a crystalline body experience or upgrade. It's hard to say what other peoples' experiences have been or how they might describe it; I can only imagine what they felt in those moments. For me, it was clearly an extremely direct and physical experience and the message was "crystal" clear. My physical body, down to every last tiny molecule of me, had changed. There was no part of me that had been left untouched.

Let's take a minute to ground in where we are in my journey. I had been through the initiation, the first steps in finding the divine light. I had purged myself of the black dragons, the guardians of my inner light. I had a rebirth, a cleaning of my human vessel. My body had been upgraded to operate in a new vibration. I had been given a vision of my future self. And now I was starting my journey toward that future. The transformation that I had already experienced at this point was truly mind-boggling, beyond any of my wildest dreams or thoughts. I had been gifted with transformation of my mind, body, and spirit. There was no part of me or my life that had been left untouched.

CHAPTER 9

Finding My Gifts

During my journey, I was given specific gifts. I have condensed the stories that spanned across multiple ceremonies to help streamline the evolution of each of them for you. While the events overlapped, I find them easier to understand when described individually.

Becoming a Healer

As I worked through each of my ceremonies and consulted with my guides and teachers, I had been experiencing moments where I was jumping over into another person's experience or I was able to move energy in ways that made little sense to me. In some cases I was able to literally see the energy move around and through a room in bright colorful waves. In other experiences, I was able to see where people were in their journeys in a picture or movie format. The first few times I experienced these, I was simply along for the ride. It was as if the work was being done with my body and energy, but I had little control over the steps or outcome of what was happening. I was the vessel or tool that some other entity was working with.

You have probably picked up on my personality a little by now in reading my story, so it might not surprise you that my coping mechanism was to dig in and do some research. My inquisitive nature took over, I rolled up my sleeves, and I started reading and watching anything I could to find any explanation for what I was experiencing. I reached out to Reiki Masters and took courses to fine-tune my abilities. Yet each time I would go back into ceremony or even into that energetic space while meditating, I would find new ways of working that would be shown to me. In retrospect, I was in a bit of a masterclass on energy healing that was being taught to me by the Universe.

I was fairly confused by what I was learning and how it all fit together. You can imagine the thoughts that I was having, going from living a linear life where there were rules and accepted truths of reality into a world where magic exists. More than a few times I thought that I might be going crazy.

And then I started to see souls in need. (Just as an aside for some context, I think of souls as the part of your spirit that resides in your human body. I think of a person's spirit as an all-encompassing being that includes your soul but is much bigger and more expansive.) The souls that I was seeing were in dire need. I believe that is why I was seeing them—they were desperate for help, and they knew (even though I didn't) that I could help them.

The souls that I was seeing were flat, so flat that they were nearly completely translucent and unable to intake or hold any real breath. For those first few that I encountered, I was so panicked at their state that I simply took to action to save them. I found myself digging a soul out from under endless piles of bricks, only to realize later that these bricks were energetic trauma that had been laying heavy on her soul, weighing her down and causing her to not be able to breathe life back into herself.

The second soul I encountered was flat and paper-thin. He was attempting to stand, but couldn't because he was too thin to support himself. I tried to help him. I would gently lift his head up and, just as he seemed to be stable, I would let go and he would fold at the waist yet again. I wondered what could help him stand on his own. I attempted several different ideas, the last of which was to pin him up with a little pushpin. He yet again folded over. With that last attempt, I let him be. We later discussed this interaction and he confirmed that he was there in the experience and understood the work that we had done. We talked at length about how he could stand taller in his everyday life and allow more breath to fill him and support him. I do check in on him periodically and he is doing well.

After several of these encounters, I started to piece together the commonalities of the process. It was clear that I was removing energetic and emotional burdens and blocks from these peoples' souls. And, while what I was doing was helpful and pretty profound for me, I also realized that there was more to healing their actual souls than simply removing the blocks and burdens that were suffocating them. I could help them jumpstart the process and create a little space or room for them to work within. But the hard work of bringing their spirits back to life and welcoming them into their bodies? That, each person had to do for themselves. Each person would have to take the opportunity, use the space that was created while the weights were removed, to breathe new life back into themselves, into their souls and spirits. For many this work continues, but for some it is just as easy for them to allow new weights, new bricks, new blocks to form.

The appearance of those first souls, flat like pancakes that would soon become so thin that they would disappear altogether, was a very visual representation to me of what people experience when their inner light dims, when they lose the fire to experience life. I had often wondered what souls look like in people who had lost all passion for living. Are their souls simply gone? Do they eventually vanish? A part of me hopes that I never find out.

Since those initial encounters with spirits that have souls that are in dire need, I have seen and worked with many other spirits. And, to my great relief, most people have quite healthy spirits and robust souls. They are often slightly detached or hovering just around their human bodies. On special occasions, I get to see people who are completely aligned with themselves. Their spirits fill their bodies completely.

It was only after many of those healing encounters that I have come to find the true importance of our breath. We breathe life into our spirits. It is what keeps them alive and healthy. It is part of our job as humans to breathe, not just to keep our bodies alive, but with intention to allow spirit into our bodies. The breath is critical to allow spirit in. It is not just taking a breath to sustain the oxygen in our bodies; there is something spiritual that happens when we breathe with intention. That air we breathe feeds our cells, but it also feeds our soul.

I believe that our spirits come to this dimension to experience, to feel all of the highs and lows, to feel the emotions, and literally to feel physical matter. In order to do that, our spirits have to be present in our bodies and alive in a healthy way. With our human sovereignty we get to make the choice of just how much of that spirit we allow to manifest within us. We get to choose how much space and intention we give.

Consider this: the word "spiritual" originates from the Latin word "*spiritus*," meaning "breath of life." The type of healing that I perform, that I have been gifted to share, is healing to allow the breath of life back into your body. The actual "healing" is the removal of blocks, obstacles, or weights that limit or inhibit the spirit from breathing life. And those blocks can be just about anything, but most often are the emotional baggage that we carry with us, buried deep inside, that cause our limiting beliefs. As we continue to hide who we truly are, pushing away the truth we feel inside, we are essentially depriving our souls, our spirits, from experiencing this existence. Healers can support the removal of those energetic blocks, but it will always remain up to the receiver to take that deep, cleansing breath and breathe life back into your core existence, to acknowledge your own spirit and nurture it.

The Seer

"How small is this visible spectrum? Imagine a reel of movie film representing the entire electromagnetic spectrum stretching the whole length of the Mississippi from its source in

Lake Itasca in Minnesota to its outflow into the Gulf of Mexico. In one of those curiously anthropomorphic facts it seems that the 'visible' section of the reel of film is almost exactly in the middle. In our Mississippi analogy this would be in Pike County about fourteen miles south-east of Hannibal, Missouri. The visible spectrum would be a single frame of film, around one inch. This is all the human eye can see out of the whole 'light' spectrum."

This amazing excerpt is from Anthony Peake's *The Infinite Mindfield*. It gives substance to the bounds in which we live. I have known that there is "more," with increasing awareness and fidelity. However, just how much more there is was beyond measure for me. Using the electromagnetic spectrum as a baseline measurement of light, it is shockingly clear that we live our lives in a tiny square of what truly exists around us.

I had already been pondering what the world looks like to animals that can see different ranges of light. For example, there is a frog that can see particular bands of light that essentially shift its reality, as if it is wearing night vision goggles all of the time, and a bee that is able to see UV light, which we can really only feel and know the results of when we sit in it for too long. I have imagined what our world would look like if I had the ability to see like these animals.

This brings me to the second gift that I have received. It is the ability to see. I see and experience life differently now, much like the frog and the bee do. I have tapped into a part of me that is able to literally see and experience parts of the spectrum that is around us always. It is a part of the spectrum that is not always obvious to everyone, but I have no doubt that this capability lays dormant in all of us. The best way that I can describe my own experience is that I can see things happen in a space that is not apparent in daylight, and those things glow as if I'm wearing night vision goggles at night. And sometimes I see things as if watching a movie of a future time.

It took me a while to put all of this into context for myself. I struggled to understand just what was happening to me and, to be honest, I wondered if there was something amiss with my actual vision for a while. But what I discovered is that, when your awareness and consciousness start to expand, the world and universe that you are able to see and understand expands too. The world and universe are bigger than what we see and experience with our basic five senses. As I became more and more in tune with my ability to feel the energy that is around us all the time, I was able to capture information and see beyond the obvious.

The real magic in having the gift of the Seer is that, at the core of it, I get to just see you. I see people as their truest selves; I work hard to acknowledge them and all that they have to offer in their totality. In the fast-paced world that we live in, it has become rare for anyone to really take the time to pause and see others. And, in the same way, so many of us no longer feel truly seen. By placing intention on seeing and understanding someone at a higher fidelity than most throughout our busy days and taking the time to feel into the energy around someone, I am able to uncover bits of information. And the truth is that, often, the people that I work with are moving so far through their own lives that they don't even see those things about themselves.

One of my favorite definitions of a Seer comes from the Mystical Shaman card deck by Alberto Villodo and Colette Baron-Reid.

> "The Seer represents the capacity to reach beyond the obvious details in life, into the Hidden Realms where information is available to those with the discernment to perceive it. This symbol represents psychic perception, intuition, and the capacity to know something without prior exposure. The Seer knows truth, always seeks truth beyond all else, and sees reality as it truly is without judgment. The Seer can read between the lines and understand what is not being said. (S)he represents the power of clarity and being able to recognize patterns."

This definition rings true to me. For me, the "see-ing" is the foundation of the healing that I am able to offer. It is the combination of these two gifts that allows me to help so many. Because I am able to see someone in their wholeness—to understand their spirit, body, and mind—I am able to discern the components and assess the connections between them. When the blocks are not as obvious, the gift of seeing allows me to find the hidden blocks, burdens, and blind spots to support the process of healing.

These gifts that I received for others were also given to me. Along with the ability to heal and see other peoples' spirits, I was able to start to see and heal my own. What I found is that there is no greater gift that I have found than to truly know yourself, to see yourself for who and what you truly are. This knowing of yourself unlocks the bounty of the Universe. Knowing yourself allows you to see the entirety of yourself, to accept yourself in a new and profound way, and learn to truly love who you are and the gifts you bring to the world.

❖

CHAPTER 10

Returning to the Path

I have to be honest with you, but mostly with myself. Throughout my journey, I had been holding on to this idea that at some point I might return to corporate life. I knew that it was not aligned with who I am, but I had a hard time really cutting the final ties to that part of my identity and closing off any of the options that I still had to return. However, I finally found the courage and updated my online profile. The first problem that I encountered was what I was going to update my title to. Any of the things that I could think of to put out there felt like they would be "too much" for people from my corporate life to take in. My biggest concern was that they would think that I had gone crazy. Maybe that was a little of my own concern peeking through. *Had* I gone crazy?

I mean, who leaves a high-paying job at the height of their career? And to chase self-enlightenment, no less? I remember living in that corporate world and what I had thought of the people who left for greener pastures, doing things much more culturally accepted than what I had left to do. I mean, I had scoffed at the women who left to go teach yoga or stay home with their kids. I thought that they just couldn't cut it. All of those judgmental thoughts that I had had about all those other people came flooding back to me. I was judging myself and paying the price for my past transgressions. I can appreciate that now. I also knew that I had to work through those shadows to release them before I could move forward.

I had to take the leap and put myself out there. I know that what you show as your job title on social media might seem like a silly little detail that is actually not that important, but for me, it is the outlet that I had to speak my truth of who I now was in that moment. It was the only platform I had where the people who knew me as the high-performing executive received updates about me.

I went to that place of bargaining with myself. I told myself that if I just didn't update my profile then I could someday return and say, "Just kidding! I was just taking a little break. I'm back!" But deep down, I knew that's not what I wanted. What I wanted was to stand fully in who I am; I just had to find that courage to let go of the self-judgment. This act was one of defiance, one that was cementing me to the path that I was walking.

As I hit "save" on my new profile, it was then that I expected a wave of embarrassment and regret to hit me. Shockingly, it didn't come. What came instead was a feeling of freedom that I hadn't felt before. It was the freedom to be myself and to actually have the chance to share my own evolution with others. I have no doubt that the people who truly respected me in my past roles will hold genuine excitement for me as I continue to step forward on this path. I felt that freedom and joy that came from proclaiming and owning exactly who I am and what I can give back to the world. I took those feelings of knowing with me as I stepped into my future. It was the signal that the Universe had been waiting for to give me my next evolution. Side Note: I'll let you in on a secret. You are so much more than your corporate job. I cannot think of a single person in my life who reacted in a negative way to the changes I have made in my life. It was (and still sometimes is) all in my own head. I am human, after all. It is, however, a universal truth that people love other people, not job titles.

CHAPTER 11

Mystical Experiences

It had been nearly a full year since that first ceremony with the shaman and my guides. The world was in an entirely new space, one that none of us could have ever imagined: we were about three months into a global pandemic that had rocked everyone's reality to its core. The people of the world could no longer go about life as usual, no matter what that life looked like to us—good or bad. We were forced to take a closer look at what was important to each of us and how we would start to restructure our own personal lives and society at large. It felt as if the world and humanity itself needed this reset, even at the cost of global upheaval.

So it was in this environment, with the world coming to a standstill, with the state of mind that we are being forced (for the better) to change, that I returned for my next set of experiences and lessons. I entered a new space for ceremony, one with far fewer people and much more space between each of us to adhere to safety measures. Unlike the previous space, which was cozy and intimate, this new space was a large room with a wall of doors that opened to the lush forest outside. We were set up in each of the corners of this room with long expanses between each of us. It was a new environment and took me a minute to get settled.

I had come with the intention to explore knowledge and wisdom. We will see where I landed. That first night started out full of play and fun. I dropped into my experience and transformed into a ball of pure energy. I was the purest form of energy; I was love. As I transcended the bounds of the human dimension, I entered into a place of pure love. In many ways, this place looked much like heaven is depicted in movies. There were endless cloud-like forms with just hints of light pink and baby blue filling in the edges. I had a felt sense that I was on a playground of sorts, like I was on the field where children experienced joy and happiness. Just as I had that thought and started to wonder where I was exactly, a group of beautiful angels discovered me. Now, I say "beautiful" because that is the feeling that they evoked, but in my experience they were actually formless concentrations of energy. I am not sure how I knew, but I was sure that they were angels; there was just a knowing that occurred.

Remember, I was energy in ball form as well. The next thing I knew, they literally picked me up and started to play with me, tossing me back and forth. After several minutes of this, which felt like hours in some ways but also timeless, like a split second, in others, they set me down and disappeared back to wherever they had come from. As a parting gift, they gave me knowledge. Not specific knowledge, just generally any knowledge that I would like to know. It came to me in the form of every book ever written being crammed into my head. It was an almost physical sensation of the books being downloaded into my mind. It was like each book was the size of an atom and all of the books ever written could fit in a single cell in my mind. I remember wondering what book I would read first and how I would ever get through reading all of them.

Leaving laughter in their wake, the angels left me with this critical piece of information: "You can read every one (of those books), but they all say the same thing. Love yourself and you will heal the world." I started to open each book, but on every page they said the same thing: they all said "love." I frantically opened more and more of the books and, sure enough, every single page said "love." At first, I thought that it must be some kind of cruel joke, to gift me every book and have them only say "love," but when I thought about this some more, it hit me that all of the lessons come back to the same thing: there is only love. I can read for the rest of my life and still will only find love.

The following morning, I felt completely in my body, productive and enjoying every aspect of just being human. It was as if a new awareness of my own flesh and ability to do "everyday things" flooded my mind and fused into my soul. I felt one with my spirit and had a new appreciation for the tasks that I had chosen for myself. I had a new knowing from my visit to heaven that I was an eternal spirit, that I am just visiting this time and space in this particular body. The experience with the angels made it so clear to me that we are truly made of energy. We are spirits made of energy, and that energy is love.

There was an awareness that came about after I touched realms beyond our own, when I was able to truly remember who and, more importantly, *what* I am. The feeling of being a spirit is pure weightlessness. You and I are pure light when we are in that realm and, as such, the ability to feel is unavailable to us. Being pure light, we are able to see everything, all permutations of time and space, and everything makes perfect logical sense. A transgression that you experienced yesterday all of a sudden fits into the expanse of all time and space, across all dimensions. The emotions are removed because every last detail fits into the divine plan that you can now see so clearly. We are only light and there is only perfection.

As I returned to my body, there was a new urgency to really feel the world around me and to feel myself. I found myself just touching my hands, rubbing them together to feel the solid nature of them. I rode my bike and let myself sweat to feel my heart beating, blood pumping, to simply feel the miracle that the human body is when it is at work. The gift of that night was the understanding that the universe is made up of pure divine energy and that is magical. But here on Earth, we get the unique gift to feel, to be, to make choices. And all of that includes the highs and the lows, the triumphs and the failures.

I moved into the second night of the ceremony with clear intentions—for love, wisdom, and healing. I spent much of that night working through relationships with my own family and relationships that others in the room were processing. This wasn't the first time that I had worked with others in the space of ceremony, but it felt much more intentional this time around. I would start with one person and help them through healing their relationship with their son, while at the same time shedding new light and perspective on my relationships with my own. Then I would move on to the next person and work through the relationship to Mother, both theirs and mine.

Moving through the room one by one, we were shifting the energy of the individual and the whole. And in between each person and archetypal relationship, I was receiving what I can only call divine gifts. The first of these gifts was the opening of the crown of my head, connecting to an energy or power source. I imagine this is what it might feel like when people reference the opening of the crown chakra; however, this felt intense rather than calm and peaceful. It felt as if my head had been plugged in to an outlet with the current running in both directions, in and out of my body. The second of these gifts was the disassembly and reassembly of my neck, back, and shoulders, but with a little added space in between. I still have not fully deciphered the meaning of this added space, but I do know that part of my body is a powerful conduit of energy. It also happens to be where energetic wings connect into your physical body.

The final gift that I received that evening was the ability to see into other peoples' experiences and help them process their own energetic blocks and spiritual burdens. This wasn't the first time that I had experienced this gift, but it was the night that it became solidified in my awareness and that I felt like I truly understood what was happening. Being further out from the experiences now and having had the time to process what was really happening, I believe that there are two main components (and likely hundreds more minor components). The first component is the ability to see into another person's experience (I now know that to be the ability to simply see another person's soul or spirit). The second is the ability to move or shift energy that is in their space or attached to them.

To clarify, I don't typically journey through all of the ins and outs of the details of another person's experience. But I do tend to check on each person's spirit to ensure they are doing well on their own and provide any aid that is requested. Through all of this work, I was learning volumes of knowledge about myself. And yet, I had no idea what was coming next.

CHAPTER 12

Meeting Myself

The next night I came into ceremony aware of the changes that were happening all around me. It felt as if the entire world had tilted on its axis to create space for this awakening and healing of so many forgotten yet critical details. What came next was nothing like I had expected.

As we came to the completion of the second night and phones were turned back on, information started to flood in that our city was in a mandatory lockdown due to unrest. There were reportedly protests and riots going on, but we had little information about anything else. It felt like we came back into a different world than the one that I had unplugged from just a few short hours earlier. I was having a hard time sorting through the details of what was going on and finding my footing. All I could think was that love could solve this all.

I didn't know this at the time, but this was the first night of over one hundred consecutive nights of protests and riots in our city, all for the ultimate goal of gaining equality and the dissolution of the systematic racism that plagues our society and government. We were in the middle of a global pandemic and the death of George Floyd had just sparked a global reckoning with the systematic racism embedded in so many of our governments. The timing of these events is not lost on me. The veils were thin and the pieces were being put into place to bring about healing and unity within our lifetimes.

We discussed not returning the following evening. However, there is a strong belief that when you set ceremony over a specific time period, the experience is orchestrated to manifest over that time period. We believed that the finale of this lesson was yet to be seen. The feeling in the space as we returned that next day was fragile and a bit unsure. With seeming chaos happening around the country and the world, were we where we were supposed to be?

I am sure it *was* where I was destined to be. My experience that night was built on the previous two. I was aligned and aware of the blessing it was to be here on Earth at this precise moment in time. That night I became Mother Earth, I became Gaia. My amnesia cleared and, just as I had seen others' spirits in previous ceremonies, I was able to see my own.

To my surprise, my spirit was not the picture of youthful beauty that I may have imagined. No, she was an old, old woman, ancient really. She walked hunched over with a crooked little wooden walking stick. Her skin was deeply wrinkled and looked like the bark of a tree. She had silvery white hair and just a hint of a knowing smile. Her innate wisdom radiated out from her.

With the chaotic energy swirling from the social unrest and this newfound connection to my own powerful self, I got to work healing. I spent what felt like a lifetime shifting energy and moving pieces. And when I could do no more, exhausted, I realized that we can heal for lifetimes. All of us can gather and continue to heal, but we don't have to. We have this amazing gift of human sovereignty; we can make the choice to be done healing. We can come together and proclaim that we are healed. We are done living in the past where that hurt and pain was created. We can make the choice to live our lives in this new day— today. We create the world that we live in. By living in the present we can heal the old wounds and move forward into the creation of this new Earth.

As I made that decision, I was able to see into a new vibration where there is heaven on Earth. It was a magical experience for me to witness the harmony that is possible and that I know will come.

That glimpse into our future can feel far-off, especially if you are reading this as we still struggle through the shedding of the old paradigm. However, I believe that Spirit has set the course, and the work needed in the cosmic divine is complete. It is now a matter of the physical world catching up to the cosmic healing. We cannot expect to see the entirety of humanity to adjust and change behavior in an instant. It will take time for the systems to adjust to this new vibration. I have a distinct note from that night that it will take years for us to see this new vibration fully manifest, but we shouldn't lose hope. Results and changes will start to surface and be seen in the next two years.

The funny thing about meeting your own spirit is that, when you do that, your spirit is most likely outside of your own body. This didn't occur to me at first, and it didn't cross my mind until I felt my spirit reenter my body. What is odd about this is that I don't recall feeling my spirit leave my body, but she clearly did in order to end up standing in front of me. And, likely because I was not aware of her leaving my body, I actually did not know who I was meeting at first. Maybe this was intentional, as the meeting of my own spirit was jarring enough once all the pieces fell into place and I realized what exactly was transpiring. In those initial meetings, I remember wondering who this ancient spirit was and why she was coming to engage with me. I clearly had lessons to learn from her and I viewed her as a teacher or ascended master of sorts that had come to help me along on my own journey.

Even after I felt her return within me, I thought that maybe I was holding another spirit within my body. But, after some time passed, I slowly realized that this woman who I was building a relationship with was me. It makes sense that, after such a long time being disconnected from my own spirit, I would need to take small steps to reconnect with myself. When we meet someone new, we are used to an introduction, then a slow creation of the relationship and the building of trust. Finally, when we are comfortable with that new person, they become a friend and part of our inner circle. My spirit knew, or rather I knew, that I needed this human construct of relationship-building into order to be comfortable and accepting of myself.

Our interactions felt awkward and a little unstable at first. I was swinging back and forth in a pretty dramatic fashion. I went from feeling "normal," like who I have always known myself to be, a human with very human experiences, to swinging to the other extreme, to being a deeply knowledgeable spirit with the perspective and wisdom of lifetimes. It felt like months passed as I bounced back and forth between these two polarities. It was at the height of this back-and-forth that one of my trusted guides and teachers offered me this: "Your spirit chose to have this experience in your body. It is through you that you breathe new life into her. You don't have to become her; you are her fountain of youth."

My guide pushed me to integrate my spirit back into my body. She pushed me to think about the situation and what was happening in a completely new way. Instead of simply accepting my spirit and becoming the ancient being, my guide encouraged me to use my current human experience to expand into what we could become together. So instead of just becoming an old woman and feeling like I couldn't stand, I could use my youthfulness (in relative terms) and passions to bring the two ends of the spectrum together.

It was challenging to accept my role in the process. I found it hard to accept that I had something to give in this relationship, that the current me was just as important as this ancient wise spirit. Eventually, though, I came to a place of understanding and acceptance. It was through me, in this human form, that my spirit could become young again, that she could operate through me, but only if I accepted her fully into my body. I needed—and she needed me—to fully allow myself to embody her, to become one. And to do that I needed to allow the integration of both of us together, not so one could take over the other but to create a new version of both of us.

After our introduction and a slow reconstruction of our relationship, it was only then, when I had built enough trust in my spirit—and myself—that I was able to bring her close enough to be in my inner circle. The irony of this was not lost on me. It is a hard moment when you realize that the emotional work that you have been doing is to learn to trust yourself. It is hard because that means that at some point in your life you lost faith in your own being. I had lost faith in myself. However, the process of rebuilding the foundation of knowing and loving who I am was what allowed me to feel solid in my connection to spirit.

By this point, I felt fully connected and open to my own spirit. I was able to grasp the true power of embodying my spirit completely. I had this feeling that something big was building, that the energy around me was shifting. But I could not figure out if there was some other part of me that I needed to dig deep into or what exactly was happening. Then, all of a sudden, I felt my spirit reenter my body. I knew that this time was different, that she would be more ingrained in my human being. The experience was beyond what I could have imagined as a possibility. Even after the rest of my experiences, I would never have guessed that this was possible. The best way that I can describe what happened is that my spirit came into my body at supersonic speed. The force as she hit my body was unlike anything I have ever experienced. My body flew forward and brought me from sitting to down on my hands and knees. I could feel every molecule in my body, as if there was a chemical reaction taking place, or maybe an energetic exchange and bonding happening within each molecule. It was the energy of my spirit and the physical energy that created my human body bonding and becoming one.

I distinctly remember that I sat back up and looked around to see if anyone else had noticed the cosmic shift that had just taken place. Based on the feeling that I had just experienced, I half expected the room to be shaken and disheveled as if a tornado or bomb had just come through. I needed some reassurance that the world around me was still stable and that I was still recognizable to the outside world. As I started to engage with the people around me, they had seen that something big had just happened to me; they simply had no way of knowing the depth of what that was.

MEETING MYSELF

✦

CHAPTER 13

Lost in the Spiritual Realm

Moving through life knowing that you are a new version of yourself is an odd feeling. For me, the way in which I was interacting with the elements and people in my life felt foreign, almost as if the ancient part of me was experiencing this dimension of Earth for the first time in a while, and needed to get used to the oddity of physical matter and existence. Yet there was something reassuring and peaceful about the mental place that I was in during this time.

I was aware that I had progressed from completely lost in the material world to possessing a knowledge of this other way of being, to knowing, to believing, and now I was embodying my own spirit. It had been a long journey and it felt like I had made it. It felt like I needed to embrace this new existence.

The best way that I can describe what I was going through was that I was a little high on my newfound spiritual awakening. The entire world seemed to make sense to me. Everything was love, everything had its divine purpose, and I saw the world as rosy and beautiful. I found myself struggling to understand why everyone couldn't see what I saw. I was struggling to relate to my friends and family who were still operating in a world of challenges and struggle. I was living in complete bliss, kind of. What I had gained in spiritual awareness, I had lost in connection and empathy.

I found that I had started to isolate myself, even more than I had previously. The less I felt I had in common with the people around me, the more I pulled further and further away and inside myself. Don't get me wrong though, it was a lovely place to be, spending so much of my time connected into the spiritual realm. It felt safe and peaceful. To be honest, it was exactly what I needed at that point in my life.

I often look back at this time period and am filled with an overwhelming sense of gratitude for just how the universe works, how Spirit gives you just the right things in the exact order that you need them. I needed to have the experience of being intrinsically connected to Spirit at that time so that I had a solid foundation for what the next several months would bring.

I had journeyed back to myself. The more attuned I became to myself, the more isolated I was from the people around me, including my husband. It is during this same time that I was growing and expanding that I was also growing apart from my husband. In many ways we were complete strangers at this point. He was steeped in a high-stress job every day, trying to manage the abrupt changes that the pandemic and social distancing had thrust upon the organization he worked for. Then, just as he might have been able to come up for air, he was confronted with the challenge of how to address racial inequality lurking within his own organization. On both a personal and work plane, I can only imagine the tension that was encapsulating him. The overwhelming stress was isolating him, and my own transformation had isolated me. Instead of coming together in these difficult times, we found ourselves the furthest we had ever been from one another.

We had both come to the realization that we no longer had the strong foundation we once had. And even though I could see our spirits together and know their long history and journey, I had to come to accept that might not be enough to save our marriage in this lifetime. It's a funny thing to know the plan, to feel the truth deep inside of you, and to also have to accept the realities of this world. It felt like my external reality and my internal mind were being ripped in two. I was losing my grip on what thoughts and information I could really trust and believe, because if my marriage to my soulmate, which I had seen so clearly, was failing, then what else that I had seen might be false too? I spent weeks wrestling with this, desperately trying to find solid ground as my life shifted under my feet. Just as I hit my lowest point, the two of us trying to hold it together for our kids as we spent our agreed upon allocated hour of family time together in the evening, the phone rang.

As soon as I heard the sound, the energy that encompassed the entire room shifted and can only be described as eerie. Before my husband even answered the phone, we were all on high alert. Chills ran down my spine as the phone connected, and a million different scenarios started to run through my mind as we heard my husband's mother's pain reverberate through our living room. Of all of the scenarios that ran through my mind, never once did I hit on the truth. Something had happened to my husband's brother, a stroke maybe, but it was unclear, and he was being taken to the emergency room.

Nothing made sense. My husband's brother was only forty-six, and he was the fittest and healthiest person any of us knew. He had competed in nineteen Ironmans, many of them at the world championships in Kona. I thought there had to be some mistake. My own mother had just had two mini strokes the summer before and she had recovered completely. I told myself, and anyone who would listen, that he would be fine.

Hours wore on and more details became available. There was bleeding on his brain, and he was going into emergency surgery. We stayed up that night on vigil in a shocked daze. I tapped into every last piece of knowledge and power that I had learned in my spiritual quest. I begged and tried to make deals with any form of spirit that would listen that night. As

I sat in bed next to my husband, waiting on news of the outcome of the surgery, I closed my eyes and watched the operating room fill with angels, more than seemed could fit, and witnessed my husband's father, who had passed when he was a child, come to support his brother. I turned to my husband and shared the vision I had just had. He wanted to know what it meant, but I didn't know. I only saw the angels and his dad arrive in the operating room; I had not witnessed any of them leaving. I had no knowledge of where his brother's spirit was.

The doctors were able to keep his body alive that night. They had found that there was massive bleeding on his brain but were unable to find or stop the bleeding. He had multiple heart failures during the surgery, so they got his body back to a stable place and put him on life support. There was nearly a week of both hope and despair until his body was stable enough to run more diagnostics. Unfortunately, he passed away a few days later with the family by his side.

I learned many powerful lessons from his passing. I learned that no one person is more powerful than the Divine plan. I learned that it doesn't matter how much you know of the spiritual realm or how aligned you are, that we cannot change certain outcomes. And I would learn in the months ahead that, even though you cannot possibly understand why certain things happen, you can learn, grow, and expand from them. We had held on and we fought to save him, to bring him back. But, in many ways, I believe his spirit was already gone, that his father and the flock of angels had come to to greet him and guide him to the other side.

My own way to process the grief was to dig in deeper and deeper to this place where he had gone. I wanted to connect to the spiritual realm and gain understanding of why things like this happen, to understand why we come to earth to experience things like this and what happens after we die.

In some ways the grieving brought my husband and I closer together. We were back to fighting a common enemy, the pain of loss. But as we traversed our own way, the problems that we had set aside only came back stronger. I had rekindled my desire to know more. I thought that if I knew more or experienced more, that I could heal my own pain, that I could heal my husband's pain, and that I could heal our relationship. I thought wrong.

CHAPTER 14

Coming Back to My Body

I had pushed myself to the edge and then, through pain, found my way back into myself. 2020 was the most difficult year of my life—it was a reckoning with all of the parts of me that I had left untended as I lived the life I thought I was supposed to be living. There were external events that rocked my world, all of our worlds—a global pandemic, economic collapse, and a reckoning with social inequalities, systematic racism, and radicalized extremists. But it was the depth that I traveled to truly find myself and integrate the pieces that I found back into a whole that defined this time in my life.

To be perfectly honest with you, I got a little lost this past year. I swung so far into the depths of my soul that I forgot for a while that I am also here, human, and that I was created to live a life of joy, grace, and connection. I was like the yogi who sits on the busy streets of India, content to be meditating as the chaotic world flies by, so completely entranced by the spiritual world that the material and physical world almost disappears. While I didn't spend quite that much of my time meditating and I did not renounce all of my worldly possessions (although I did contemplate it), I did travel so far to the edge that I almost lost the only things that are important to me— the connection that I have with my husband and kids, the connection I have with the people and the spirits that mean the most to me.

I learned more than I could have imagined and I have now integrated much of those learnings back into the whole of myself. The capstone of my journey so far has been the realization that none of the Spiritual matters in this exact moment, if I don't live this life that I have right now to the absolute fullest I can. I know all about the Spiritual realm; I can travel there and be there for as long as I want, but if I get lost again and spend too much of my precious time that I have on this Earth there, then I am missing out on the whole point of having a life— the human experience.

It has taken me some time and a whole lot of work to come back to realize something that, ironically, I already knew. Each of us has to experience our own lives, and we have to walk that journey ourselves. When I returned to understanding and believing this and allowing the space for all of us to heal it created a cosmic chain reaction. The shadow, the dark emotions that had been clinging so desperately to our marriage slowly started to fall away. The more that each of us took steps into our new future, whatever that was going to be, the ugliness and resentment of the past fell away and faded. It freed us to embrace each present moment for exactly what it was—effort and love.

After the long journey of breaking myself free of the cage of limiting beliefs that I had created for myself as well as many, many nights spent doing the hard work of digging deep into the depths of my soul to find myself, it is now that I can truly appreciate how all of the pieces of my life experience fit together to allow me to be here now. I can appreciate the lows for what they really were, stepping-stones in my life to help me return to my divine self, to help me know and see my own divine light within. I can see and appreciate how loss and suffering in our lives helps us to grow and expand. How it gives us the capacity to love more and love more deeply. I can embrace the fact that I will never know or understand everything that happens, and that the things that happen in our lives are just as they should be.

I sit here in complete gratitude as I take my first steps into the next leg of my journey—the part where I live my life to the fullest it can be lived, finally connected to the people who I love and who matter most to me: my husband, my children, and my family. This is the part where I have returned to my body, embodying my divine spirit—not as something to be endured, but as the temple that we all know our bodies to be. Cherishing my body as the temple in which my Spirit goes to worship and learn, to expand and experience. In the spiral nature that is everything, I return once again to the place that I started, just slightly beyond the last starting point and infinitely more aware. I am looking forward to the growth and expansion that this next cycle brings me.

CHAPTER 15

Finding 5D

And so here I am now, back in this amazing human body that I have actively chosen to live in, this temple for my spirit to reside in to experience this dimension of Earth—the time, space, connection, love, disappointment, sorrow, and suffering. I have been full circle (or full spiral, if you will) and I am back to living life. However, in this revolution, I am experiencing all that is at a new, slightly different vibration.

That vibration is what allows me to see the world that we all live in with slightly different sight. That sight that I have been gifted, and that is completely accessible to you too, is viewing all that is, knowing that there is a source, something greater than each of us individually. We are all a part of the divine energy that is driving, managing, and creating this experience. And that being, that source, Spirit, the

Universe, the Divine, it is only love. So anything that is happening in this dimension can only be in service of love as well.

Maybe you are wondering how you get to this place, how you find the perspective that I reference. It is a paradox, as most things are with Spirit. The perspective is gained as we come back to trust and surrender, belief and faith. It is in the simplicity of these acts that we can find the most comfort. When we can trust that there are spiritual beings that are on our side supporting us, that we are spiritual beings that cannot fail, it transforms every way that we approach the experience of life.

If you can wrap your head around the fact that we are spirits—in whatever way that can resonate with you—that we are made up of energy and energy cannot be destroyed, and if you can believe that we come from another realm or dimension that is not Earth, then as you work through the purpose of why we might come to Earth you might find, as I have, that there are many reasons to come here. It is a common belief that we come to learn lessons, that we are in a sort of soul school and we need to continue to pass lessons to move up in rank or status as spirits. Some even believe we come here because we are in an epic battle to save humanity or something even greater.

For me, I landed on the idea that we come to this dimension in this particular time to simply experience. And the purpose of all those experiences is to expand love. If that is the reason for the very existence of humanity and Earth, then every experience—no matter if it is "good" or "bad"—is designed to increase the total amount of love that exists in the universe.

I stay in what some call the fifth dimension, in this place of awakeness and awareness, by remembering these truths.

1. I am a spirit that has come to visit this dimension.

2. I cannot possibly know the Divine plan, so I must trust.

3. Everything that happens in my life, or the greater collective, will ultimately be for the highest and best good.

4. There is no single right way to do this.

5. The only ending to this story is to return home, to love.

I can honestly say that these core beliefs, my truths, have helped me get through deeply challenging times. They also help me get through the insignificant moments in life, those moments that used to derail my entire days for no reason.

On the level of the collective, I have been able to see the hope for the future as we lived through a global pandemic, social and political unrest, and immeasurable loss. While living through unprecedented times that have been scary and devastating for so many, these truths allowed me to see the much-needed change that would come from those sacrifices. The toll that the pandemic alone took on people globally has been truly heartbreaking; no one can argue that. However, given that many of the circumstances were out of my personal control to change, I was able to focus on the benefits that would come from the entire world having to reassess how we live our daily lives. The priorities of nearly every person shifted by the end of the pandemic, all for different reasons, but the reality is that the entire world shifted from the paradigm that we were living in. We are moving into a new construct that is still solidifying.

On a personal level, these truths allow me to flow through life with inner grace and ease. Much like many of you, I get annoyed with my children when they leave the kitchen a mess, forget to do a chore that I have asked them to do repeatedly, or do any of the hundreds of things children, spouses, life partners, family, and friends can do that are just not what you wanted. However, I now know that whatever that thing is that happened, I and we can simply flow into the next moment. I now know that it is our own choice how we react and what we make of it. Just because something, big or small, didn't happen just as I wanted it to, or in the timing that I had believed it needed to be complete, it will still be okay. It is just another confirmation that life is not a predestined series of events and that, no matter the order of the twists and turns, we still reach our final destination.

CHAPTER 16

Expanding the Universal Energy, Love

What is the final destination? That final destination is the return to love. There is no other option, no other ending to our experience here on Earth. You may be thinking that I am talking about death, but death is really just one path to returning to love. Think of love as the top of a mountain. We are all on our own paths as we climb toward the top. For some of the journey you might be following in another's footsteps, and for other parts you might be forging an entirely new path. Maybe you take the journey that spirals around and around this mountain, slowly gaining altitude with each revolution. Maybe you take the direct route and find your way to the top in a straightforward but difficult route.

The truth is that, whether you die on your journey and return to love or you reach the mountaintop, we all return home. The only difference is how much time you have left in this experience on Earth to enjoy before returning home.

The collective has shifted. More and more of us are finding our own way home. And, unlike in the past, we are sharing the way in which we got here. This sharing is not to tell you that you have to take the same path. Instead, the sharing of stories is to offer you new options, new maps, new insight to help you find your own way home back to the light and love within.

Epilogue

And so here we are, sitting in a comfortable place, wrapped up in a book. Something inspired you to pick up this book and actually read it. There is some magic that was just transfused into your being. By sharing in my story, you have reactivated your own soul knowing deep within you. For some of you, this might bring back experiences of your own awakening. For others, this might be calling on parts of you that are buried deep within you.

This book, and the work I do with clients, both serve to illuminate the parts of us that have been forgotten, neglected, or have lain undiscovered. There is magic, a transformation and healing, that takes place when we are able to reconnect to those parts. Those parts of us are reignited, they are seen, and when they are in our conscious awareness, we are able to breathe new life into them. This process of illumination, transformation, and new life gifts us the pieces that were once missing from life back to us. We are able to experience life with a new vibrancy that did not exist before. We are able to experience life from a place of wholeness, allowing us to finally understand the completeness of divinity and the Universe.

My greatest hope is that everyone can experience what it feels like to truly know yourself, to know your spirit, and to finally feel whole. Because, when you connect to and embody the wholeness of who you really are, you no longer feel like something is missing in your life. You no longer feel the need to seek. You are finally able to relax into the ease of a life divinely given. You are able to truly experience the connection, joy, and love that exists in each moment. You are able to let go, trust in divine timing, and exist in a knowing that life is unfolding to allow the highest expression of yourself.

If you have found your own wholeness, I would love to hear about your journey. If you are seeking or searching for that thing that is missing from your life and my story resonates, please reach out and engage with me. You can visit my website at dmitriaburby. com to learn more about me and upcoming content. Find me on Instagram at @luminancehealing to get my latest thoughts and visit luminancehealing.com to explore my blog and discover ways I can help you on your path. I do all of this to support your journey of self-discovery, to help you know that you are not alone on the path. I am honored that you spent this precious time with me and know that we have been brought together for a reason. Thank you for allowing me to manifest my own dreams and purpose by allowing me to plant a seed of love in your heart.

About the Author

Dmitria Burby is an author, speaker, spiritual guide, and healer. She has helped countless people reconnect with their spirits and awaken to their true power and light within. She has set out to inspire people everywhere to reflect inward to find the path to their truth, happiness, and joy. Dmitria founded Luminance Healing to create community and space for personal healing, growth, and transformation to manifest.

For more information about her, visit DmitriaBurby.com.

Made in the USA
Monee, IL
06 April 2022